DEDICATION

I do whole heartedly dedicate this
book to my precious, lovely and forever
wonderful parents: my Father the Honorable
Chief J. E. Ovbije and my mother Elder
Mrs. Margaret Orhe Edokpagha Ovbije, I
simply call my father Papa and my mother
Mama.
I cannot speak, preach or write about love
without God not bringing my parents and
my upbringing to my attention. I am forever
grateful to God for my parents.
They gave me unconditional love,
they taught me love, they taught me how to
forgive anyone who wrong me, they taught
me to never hold a grudge, they believe the
best of me, they encouraged me always, they
see greatness in me, they never speak negative of each other, or of me. They never
speak negative of anyone, they never in-
volve in gossip. They taught me how to relate to ladies, they taught me always put the
lady away from the traffic: when walking
with a lady on the street, they taught me how
to speak(there is a big differences between
speaking and talking, when you speak, you
say: read St. Mark 11:23, speaking goes

with purpose, in speaking there is focus). I remember very well as a child and into my teens, my father would ask me between intervals "what is your target" meaning what is your goal, "yes you are in holiday, but the school did not take books away from you" meaning because school is not in session does not mean you should not be reading, I learned from them, to slow to speak, to never make a statement about a thing without the knowledge of the matter, they taught me to listen, more than talking, I was very aware of the respect and dignity people in the community, in the city I grew up in and in other places, gave to my parents, yes my last name is well known, and I was taught by my parents never to tarnish it, it is like a crown, when I became a Christian, I read in the bible "A good name is rather to be chosen than riches,…" Proverbs 22:1, I thank God I never experience poverty. I do credit them for my education; they taught me the rudiment of education. They prepared the path for me to know God intimately. I am short of words.

There are not enough pages in the world for me to express the love my parents gave to me and my love for them, and all they taught me, also there are not enough pages for me to express my deepest thanks and gratitude to God for my parents.

Father God, I thank you for blessing and ordaining that I should come into this world through this wonderful parents of mine, I am forever grateful to you for my parents, in Jesus name, Amen and Amen and Amen, and a Lot of Amen.

ACKNOWLEDGMENTS

To my wonderful parents, Chief J. E. Ovbije & Mrs. Margaret O. Ovbije, and to my siblings. My father was a man that lived a life that left an excellent and lasting impression on me. Our family knew the meaning of a loving, secure and rich home because of my father's presence. I thank God for the private elementary school at Sapele: Children Nursery School, where I attended. It was there that I encounter God for the first time in prayer in a very early age.

To my precious pastor and his lovely wife, both were strong examples of a man and a woman devoted to God. I was fortunate to have pastor & Mrs. Umukoro, both disciples me. I thank them both for their daily early morning prayer life. To the men of God who also impacted my prayer life, W. F. Kumuyi and Benjamin Udi.

Finally to my sweet, precious, wonderful wife Theresa Spearman Ovbije, a woman of God, whom I simply call "sweetie".

"God's love for me is unbeatable" L. O. Ovbije.

"Because God loves me, he created things for me, not me for things" L. O. Ovbije.

"The cross of Jesus Christ answered every question about God's love for you, yes for you and me" L. O. Ovbije.

PREFACE

God's love for you is unconditional. If you have not discovered it, keep searching and don't quit. The greatest discovery you will ever make in life is the love of God for you. When you discover the love of God for you, you will forever love yourself and then you will be capable of loving people. You cannot love anybody, until you love yourself. You see in people, what you see in yourself. You are not superior to anyone, and no person is superior to you. Those that demean others, in order to make themselves important, do so as a cover for their own inferiority complex which they are struggling with in private. Religion builds hierarchy, but in Christ, all those that are born again are one. None is superior to the other. There were many religious leaders in the past, there are many religious leaders today, and there will be many religious leaders in the future. Jesus

*Christ said "I came that you may have life and have life more abundantly" St. John 10:10. He did not say "I came that you may have religion and have more religion". It is written "In him was life; and the life was the light of men." St. John 1:4, Jesus Christ and him alone paid the vicarious price for your sin that is why it is written "Jesus saith unto him, I am the way, the truth, and the life: no man cometh unto the Father, but by me." St. John 14:6, Jesus Christ is the **only** way, the truth, and the life that leads to the True and Living God.*

God created you in his own image and likeness. Of his own will he created you, of his own will he loves you. The love of God for you is not based on you or on any of your performances, nor your religious performance. There is absolutely nothing you can do to stop God's love for you. In fact there is nothing in your past, present, and fu-

ture that can stop God's love for you. That is the gospel and that is why Jesus Christ came to the earth for you, For God so love you that he gave his only begotten Son, Jesus Christ to you that if you believe on Jesus Christ, you will be saved. Believe on the God, who believes in you by sending Jesus Christ to you. Yes! You can be save right now; yes you can accept Jesus Christ right now. "Neither is there salvation in any other: for there is none other name under heaven given among men, whereby we must be saved." Acts 4:12 "And they said, Believe on the Lord Jesus Christ, and thou shalt be saved, and thy house." Acts 16:31, when you accept Jesus Christ into your heart, you accept God's love for you and the finished works of Jesus Christ for you. "That if thou shalt confess with thy mouth the Lord Jesus, and shalt believe in thine heart that God hath raised him from the dead, thou shalt be saved. For with the heart man believeth unto righteousness; and with the mouth confession is made unto salvation." Romans 10:9-10. Say boldly with your mouth "I believe with my heart, Jesus Christ is the Son of God, Jesus Christ died for my sins, buried for my transgression, rose up for my justification, right now I accept Jesus Christ into my heart and I confess with my mouth Jesus Christ is my Saviour and Lord, I am born again right now. The Spirit of the Living God is in me now and he is in me forever, Amen

WEEK ONE

Love never fails:
1 Corinthians 13:8

God Loves Me

In the beginning was the Word, and the Word was with God, and the Word was God.
St. John 1:1
Boldly Say: I boldly believe with my heart and confess with my mouth that the Bible is the word of God. In the Bible is the revelation knowledge of creation, yes! In the beginning, in the Bible is the plan of redemption for the human race, which race you and I belong, yes! Redemption is available for all through Jesus Christ of Nazareth, In the Bible is the revelation knowledge of the God whose likeness I am; In the Bible is the revelation knowledge

of God's love for me. In the Bible is the revelation knowledge of the power of love. Love never fails. The moment anyone accept Jesus Christ into their heart, that individual becomes a partaker of his divine nature. I have accepted Jesus Christ into my heart; therefore as he is so I am in this present world. These I believe, the devil which the Bible spoke about cannot deceive me through any medium to believe anything contrary to the word of God.

Jeremiah 29:11
Romans 8:35-39

NOTE:

WEEK TWO

Love never fails:
1 Corinthians 13:8

God Loves Me

In the beginning God created the heaven and the earth.

Genesis 1:1

Boldly Say: I boldly believe with my heart and confess with my mouth that God Almighty created the heaven and the earth, because it is written in the Word of God, yes the Bible, that God created the heaven and the earth. Everything in the heaven and everything in the earth and everything that is below the earth was created by God Almighty. The devil and his cohorts cannot deceive me about this matter.

According to the word of God, everything God created was good. Everything God created was created by his spoken word, but he created the human race in the beginning with his own hands and breathes his life into man. This makes me very important and special, yes above all the other creation by God.

Jeremiah 29:11
Romans 8:35-39

NOTE:

WEEK THREE

Love never fails:
1 Corinthians 13:8

God Loves Me

So God created man in his own image, in the image of God created he him; male and female created he them.

Genesis 1:27

Boldly Say: I boldly believe with my heart and confess with my mouth that I am created by God Almighty. Not only am I created by God, but God created me in his own image. That set me apart from everything else God created. I am God's master piece of his creation. I and all human beings are above every other creation God made in every dimension of existence. God has crowned me with glory and honour. God has assigned an angel to me. God has surrounded me around with favour. God has anointed me with his Holy Spirit. God has destined me with greatness.

Jeremiah 29:11
Romans 8:35-39

NOTE:

WEEK FOUR

Love never fails:
1 Corinthians 13:8

God Loves Me

And God said, Let us make man in our image, after our likeness: and let them have dominion over the fish of the sea, and over the fowl of the air, and over the cattle, and over all the earth, and over every creeping thing that creepeth upon the earth.
Genesis 1:26

Boldly Say: I boldly confess that God did not give me dominion over people, and God did not give any person dominion over me. God has given me dominion over his entire creature that is not created in his own image. God has given me dominion over the devil and all his cohorts. God has given me dominion over everything that came from the devil due to the fall of the human race.

Jeremiah 29:11
Romans 8:35-39

NOTE:

WEEK FIVE

Love never fails:
1 Corinthians 13:8

God Loves Me

I will praise thee; for I am fearfully and wonderfully made: marvellous are thy works; and that my soul knoweth right well. Psalm 139:14

Boldly Say: I am fearfully and wonderfully made by God Almighty. I am more than a number in the computer; I am more than a statistical group, I am more than the visible me people see, God is a Spirit, and He created me as a spirit being. God, yes, the Creator of Heaven and Earth, is my Father, and I boldly confess, I am his child. And there is nothing the devil or anyone can do about my confession. In fact the devil knows that I am a child of the Most High God, and the devil respect my confession, and I do enforce my confession on the devil, in Jesus name, Amen.

Jeremiah 29:11
Romans 8:35-39

NOTE:

WEEK SIX

Love never fails:
1 Corinthians 13:8

God Loves Me

For God so loved the world, that he gave his only begotten Son, that whosoever believeth in him should not perish, but have everlasting life.

St. John 3:16

Boldly Say: I believe God loves me, I believe in Jesus, I do believe with my heart and confess with mouth that Jesus Christ is the Son of God, and he is my Saviour and Lord. I believe that I am now born again. I do now possess the love of God in me. I do now love myself as

God loves me. I love people as God love people. I do now walk in the love of God. I am very love conscious, I do walk and talk in love, whatever I do in word or deed, I do it in love to the glory of Christ Jesus the Lord.

Jeremiah 29:11
Romans 8:35-39

NOTE:

WEEK SEVEN

Love never fails:
1 Corinthians 13:8

God Loves Me

And hope maketh not ashamed; because the love of God is shed abroad in our hearts by the Holy Ghost which is given unto us.

Romans 5:5

Boldly Say: I am born again, the Holy Spirit does live in me, and the love of God is in me. I love me, and I do love people. The love of God in me is greater than any opposing spirit and forces that is in the world. I love God, I love me, and I love people. I do see myself as God sees me, I do see people as God sees people, God lives in me by his Holy

Spirit, God loves people through me. I am God's ambassador on earth, I do take God's embassy with me everywhere I go, and I am God's Kingdom person.

Jeremiah 29:11
Romans 8:35-39

NOTE:

WEEK EIGHT

Love never fails:
1 Corinthians 13:8

God Loves Me

A new commandment I give unto you, That ye love one another; as I have loved you, that ye also love one another.

St. John 13:34

Boldly Say: I boldly confess I am born again by God, who is Love. I inherit love; I am made in the image and likeness of Love. I live in love, my conversation is in love, I do possess the love lifestyle of living, my God kind of love lifestyle of living which is seen by everyone I come in contact with, whatever I do in word or deed, I do it in love. Yes, I am consumed in God's love. I dare to think and relate to people from God's love arena. Yes, I love me, I love Christians, and I love Sinners.

Jeremiah 29:11
Romans 8:35-39

NOTE:

WEEK NINE

Love never fails:
1 Corinthians 13:8

God Loves Me

But the stranger that dwelleth with you shall be unto you as one born among you, and thou shalt love him as thyself; for ye were strangers in the land of Egypt: I am the LORD your God. Leviticus 19:34

Boldly Say: I was a sinner, but I accepted Jesus Christ, now I am a saint. It is by the grace of God through faith that I became born again. I am what I am by the grace of God. The same grace God gave to me and still gives to me daily; now I

am giving that same grace to others.
I love me, and I do love others, as I
love myself.

Jeremiah 29:11
Romans 8:35-39

NOTE:

WEEK TEN

Love never fails:
1 Corinthians 13:8

God Loves Me

Now before the feast of the pass-over, when Jesus knew that his hour was come that he should depart out of this world unto the Father, having loved his own which were in the world, he loved them unto the end.
St. John 13:1

Boldly Say: The love of God in Christ Jesus towards me and for me has no limit. God's love for me is unconditional. The love of God to-wards me and for me is based on himself, not on me. Therefore, I chose to enjoy my God and my Father's love. I love me unconditionally. I refuse to beat myself, if I miss the mark; I will take advantage of the provision which God who is my heavenly Father has provided for me, that provision is the precious blood of my Lord Jesus. That is, if I miss it, I will confess, and God is faithful and just to forgive me all my sins and cleanse me with the precious blood of my Lord Jesus from all unrighteousness.

Jeremiah 29:11
Romans 8:35-39

NOTE

WEEK ELEVEN

Love never fails:
1 Corinthians 13:8

God Loves Me

Who shall separate us from the love of Christ? shall tribulation, or distress, or persecution, or famine, or nakedness, or peril, or sword?

Romans 8:35

Boldly Say: **Who shall separate me from the love of Christ? No one can separate me from the love of Christ. Things visible or invisible, the devil or any of his cohorts cannot separate me from the love of God, which is in Christ Jesus my Lord. God loves me regardless who like me** or don't, I am very satisfied with the love of God for me and towards me. I boldly believe in the love God has for me, I boldly live in the love God has for me, my residence is in God's love, anyone looking for me, will find me in God's love, that is where I live. God loves me greatly and I love me greatly.

Jeremiah 29:11
Romans 8:35-39

NOTE:

WEEK TWELVE

Love never fails:
1 Corinthians 13:8

God Loves Me

We love him, because he first loved us.

1 John 4:19

Boldly Say: Any questions about God's love for me and any human being were settled on the cross by Jesus Christ. Therefore, I do not question the love of God for me or the love of Jesus Christ for me and towards me. Since God loves me and sent Jesus Christ to die on the cross for me, I accept everything his blood bought for me. I accept God's un-conditional love for me and towards me. I love God, I love Jesus, I love me, and I love people. I do not have to understand God's love for me or his love for people, but it is my privilege and his honour for me to enjoy his love for me, and to introduce others to his unconditional love.

Jeremiah 29:11
Romans 8:35-39

NOTE:

WEEK THIRTEEN

Love never fails:
1 Corinthians 13:8

God Loves Me

And I have declared unto them thy name, and will declare it: that the love wherewith thou hast loved me may be in them, and I in them.

St. John 17:26

Boldly Say: Lord Jesus, I thank you that the same love the Father has for you is in me. I am loved by my heavenly Father. Just as the Father was in you, so are you in me. As the Father was in Jesus Christ doing the miracles, signs and wonders through him, so is Jesus Christ in me today doing miracles, signs, and wonders through me, the love of God in me leads me to compel people to come to the saving knowledge of Jesus Christ, the love of God in me reaches out to the sick to heal the sick. God loves me; I love me, and God love people through me.

Jeremiah 29:11
Romans 8:35-39

NOTE:

WEEK FOURTEEN

**Love never fails:
1 Corinthians 13:8**

God Loves Me

For all the law is fulfilled in one word, even in this; Thou shalt love thy neighbour as thyself.

Galatians 5:14

Boldly Say: **I am a doer of God's word. Thy word O! God is sweeter than honey to my taste. To do thy word O! God was the purpose of my birth. To love my neighbour as myself is my fulfillment of your law. To the measure that I love myself is the measure I will love my neighbour. Therefore, I love myself with the same love God have for me, and I love my neighbour as myself. God** does delight in me loving myself. Loving me is a commandment from God. God does live in me by his Holy Spirit, God lives in me because he declares me holy, righteous, and just the very moment I accepted Jesus Christ and his finish works.

Jeremiah 29:11
Romans 8:35-39

NOTE:

WEEK FIFTEEN

Love never fails:
1 Corinthians 13:8

God Loves Me

But God commendeth his love toward us, in that, while we were yet sinners, Christ died for us.

Romans 5:8

Boldly Say: Christ died for me, while I was a sinner. God valued me, and sent Jesus Christ to pay the greatest price for my soul. Therefore, since God loves me and value me, I boldly love me and value me. Because, I love me with the love of God which is unconditional and I value me, I refuse a lifestyle that is destructive, and I say yes to God's kind of living. Since God love and value me when I was a sinner, I do love and value every human person. I am what I am by the grace of God.

Jeremiah 29:11
Romans 8:35-39

NOTE:

WEEK SIXTEEN

Love never fails:
1 Corinthians 13:8

God Loves Me

The LORD hath appeared of old unto me, saying, Yea, I have loved thee with an everlasting love: therefore with lovingkindness have I drawn thee.

Jeremiah 31:3

Boldly Say: The love of God for me and towards me is for everlasting. God loves me. I chose to love what God loves. Therefore, I chose to love me, as God loves me. I love me unconditionally, without any performance from me, without asking for anybody's approval, endorsement, and counsel. I love me and I love people unconditionally. No one have to perform to get my love.

Jeremiah 29:11
Romans 8:35-39

NOTE:

WEEK SEVENTEEN

Love never fails:
1 Corinthians 13:8

God Loves Me

Then Jesus beholding him loved him, and said unto him, One thing thou lackest: go thy way, sell whatsoever thou hast, and give to the poor, and thou shalt have treasure in heaven: and come, take up the cross, and follow me.

St. Mark 10:21

Boldly Say: Whenever, I miss the mark, Jesus Christ always reaches out to me in love and restores me to himself. Jesus Christ never condemns me when I miss the mark.

People may judge me, but Jesus Christ always reaches out to me with his love. Yes, Jesus loves me. Therefore, whenever I do miss the mark, I will run to God, I will not run from the God who loves me greatly.

Jeremiah 29:11
Romans 8:35-39

NOTE:

WEEK EIGHTEEN

Love never fails:
1 Corinthians 13:8

God Loves Me

I in them, and thou in me, that they may be made perfect in one; and that the world may know that thou hast sent me, and hast loved them, as thou hast loved me.

St. John 17:23

Boldly Say: I boldly declare I do love and accept Christians as Christ has accepted me, I do demonstrate it publicly that the sinners may know that the same love God has for Jesus, God has for me. The Father was in the Son in his earthly walk, and today Christ is in me, the hope of glory. Just as the Father was in Jesus Christ, so is Christ in me by the Holy Spirit, What the Father was to the Son, when the Son was on earth in the garment of flesh, so is the Son is to me now.

Jeremiah 29:11
Romans 8:35-39

NOTE:

WEEK NINETEEN

Love never fails:
1 Corinthians 13:8

God Loves Me

Greater love hath no man than this, that a man lay down his life for his friends.

St. John 15:13

Boldly Say: **Jesus Christ, who knew no sin, was made sin for me that I might be made the righteousness of God in Christ Jesus. I am God's righteousness in Christ Jesus. God loves me. I am accepted in the beloved, I accept myself; I love myself as God loves me. I love people, as I love me. God has invited me to come boldly to the throne of grace, I do have unlimited access to God at** any time. God is my very own Father and I am his very own child. God and I love each other, we love our company and we love to spend time together. Yes, we love to fellowshipping with one another.

Jeremiah 29:11
Romans 8:35-39

NOTE:

WEEK TWENTY

Love never fails:
1 Corinthians 13:8

God Loves Me

A friend loveth at all times, and a brother is born for adversity. **Proverbs 17:17**

Boldly Say: Father, I thank you that you love me at all times. My God does not take vacation from loving me. I am loved by God con-tinuously. There is no stopping or quitting in God's love for me. No devil, no person, no condition, no situation, I dare to say no sin, can stop God's love for me and towards me, absolutely God has never and he will never for one split second stop loving me. The same love God has for me, I do have for me, the same love I have for me I do have for people, and I am partaker of God's divine nature. Father, I praise you, forever and ever, Amen.

Jeremiah 29:11
Romans 8:35-39

NOTE:

WEEK TWENTY-ONE

Love never fails:
1 Corinthians 13:8

God Loves Me

I am crucified with Christ: nevertheless I live; yet not I, but Christ liveth in me: and the life which I now live in the flesh I live by the faith of the Son of God, who loved me, and gave himself for me.

Galatians 2:20

Boldly Say: When Jesus Christ was crucified, I was crucified with him, when he was buried, I was buried with him, when he rose from the grave, I rose up from the grave with him, and I am bone of his bone, flesh of his flesh. Jesus Christ and I are one. He lives in me, and the life which I do now live, I live by his faith. Love cannot be killed. Yes, I know in the depth of my heart that because Jesus lives, I do live also, love never fails.

Jeremiah 29:11
Romans 8:35-39

NOTE:

WEEK TWENTY-TWO

Love never fails:
1 Corinthians 13:8

God Loves Me

As the Father hath loved me, so have I loved you: continue ye in my love.

St. John 15:9

Boldly Say: I am loved by Jesus Christ, the same love the Father have for Jesus Christ, the same love Jesus Christ have for me. As the Father was with Jesus Christ in his earthly walk, so is Jesus Christ is with me now. The Father never left Jesus Christ alone until the cross, so Jesus Christ will never leave me nor forsake me. I do boldly live in Jesus Christ's love. I do boldly confess that Jesus Christ is with me always. I am never alone. For he said I will never leave thee nor forsake thee. I can boldly say the Lord is my helper, and I will not fear what man shall do unto me. God is for me and God is with me always.

Jeremiah 29:11
Romans 8:35-39

NOTE:

WEEK TWENTY-THREE

Love never fails:
1 Corinthians 13:8

God Loves Me

The LORD did not set his love upon you, nor choose you, because ye were more in number than any people; for ye were the fewest of all people:
Deuteronomy 7:7

Boldly Say: I say yes to God's love for me and towards me, not because I feel it or because I have full understanding of it, I say yes to God's love for me, for it is not based on my own righteousness, or on my good works. I say yes to God's love for me and towards me because God really love me. I say yes to God's love for me, because of his own will he chose to love me. I say yes to God's love for me because of his own will he created me in his own image and likeness. Father I thank you for the reality of your unconditional love for me. Father I thank you that I know deep in my heart and in my spirit that you love me greatly. Father I thank you for your great love for me, Father I am very grateful to you, for your love for me.

Jeremiah 29:11
Romans 8:35-39

NOTE:

WEEK TWENTY-FOUR

Love never fails:
1 Corinthians 13:8

God Loves Me

And he will love thee, and bless thee, and multiply thee: he will also bless the fruit of thy womb, and the fruit of thy land, thy corn, and thy wine, and thine oil, the increase of thy kine, and the flocks of thy sheep, in the land which he sware unto thy fathers to give thee.
Deuteronomy 7:13
Boldly Say: God loves me, because of his great love for me, he daily load me with benefits. God does bless my coming in and my go-

ing out, he has commanded his blessing to overtake me, and where ever I go, I am bless, because he is with me forever. Whatever I put my hands to do prosper, I do have God's favour on my life. I am a vessel unto honour, I am God's representative on earth, and I am Jesus Christ's ambassador on earth.

Jeremiah 29:11
Romans 8:35-39

NOTE:

WEEK TWENTY-FIVE

Love never fails:
1 Corinthians 13:8

God Loves Me

But God, who is rich in mercy, for his great love wherewith he loved us,

Ephesians 2:4

Boldly Say: God's mercy towards me is very rich, his mercy towards me are new every day. God's love for me is great, very great. God's love for me set me apart to walk and talk with him daily. I am his dwelling place. There is no force in the visible and in the invisible that can conquer us. God always cause me to triumph in Christ Jesus. God and I are unbeatable.

God and I walk together, talk to each other, and fellowship with one another every day. God and I love our daily time of fellowship. Christ and I win souls for God all the time.

Jeremiah 29:11
Romans 8:35-39

NOTE:

WEEK TWENTY-SIX

Love never fails:
1 Corinthians 13:8

God Loves Me

And to know the love of Christ, which passeth knowledge, that ye might be filled with all the fulness of God.

Ephesians 3:19

Boldly Say: I say yes to the love of Christ for me, I do not understand why Christ loves me, but I know in my heart that he loves me, and it is forever settled in my heart that Christ loves me, therefore, I say yes to his love for me. I say boldly, I love me regardless of how people feel about me or regardless of what people say about me good or bad, this I

know in the depth of my heart and
my spirit that Jesus Christ loves, I
love me and I love people regardless
of what environment they grew up
in, because everyone is created by
God in his own image and likeness.

Jeremiah 29:11
Romans 8:35-39

NOTE:

WEEK TWENTY-SEVEN

Love never fails:
1 Corinthians 13:8

God Loves Me

Behold, what manner of love the Father hath bestowed upon us, that we should be called the sons of God: therefore the world knoweth us not, because it knew him not.

1 John 3:1

Boldly Say: God loves me greatly. I say yes and thanks to God for his great love for me. Because, God loves me greatly, he sent his Son to die in my place, so that I do not have to die for my sins. O! What a great love. I boldly declare to the invisible world and the visible world that I am greatly love by God. I do belong to God. I have accepted Jesus Christ into my heart. I believe with all my heart and I boldly confess with my mouth, that Jesus Christ is my Saviour and Lord. Yes, my heavenly Father loves me greatly. Therefore, I love me and I do love everybody.

Jeremiah 29:11
Romans 8:35-39

NOTE:

WEEK TWENTY-EIGHT

Love never fails:
1 Corinthians 13:8

God Loves Me

Beloved, if God so loved us, we ought also to love one another.
1 John 4:11

Boldly Say: God loves me. I am God's child, and of his free will he created me, and recreated me. Yes, he gave birth to me by his Holy Spirit. I belong to God Almighty. God's love is in me. I do love me, I do love Christians, and I do love sinners. I love everybody because everybody is created by God Almighty. Christians and non-Christians are created by the Holy God. I am filled and charged with God's love.

I am not ordinary, I am a super being, because the God of the super-
natural does live in me by is Holy
Spirit. I refuse to underestimate
God, and what God will and can do
in me and through me. To bless human being is God's great desire and
also my great desire.

Jeremiah 29:11
Romans 8:35-39

NOTE:

WEEK TWENTY-NINE

Love never fails:
1 Corinthians 13:8

God Loves Me

And walk in love, as Christ also hath loved us, and hath given himself for us an offering and a sacrifice to God for a sweetsmelling savour.

Ephesians 5:2

Boldly Say: Yes, Jesus loves me this I know, therefore, I do walk in the love Jesus has for me, Jesus gave himself for me because he loves me, I do love Jesus therefore, I do obey him, I obey Christ by walking in his love for me. I do live by the word of God.

I do forgive myself whenever I miss the mark as Christ forgave me. I do forgive people as Christ forgave me, whenever they wrong me or sin against me. I do love me, and I do love people.

Jeremiah 29:11
Romans 8:35-39

NOTE:

WEEK THIRTY

Love never fails:
1 Corinthians 13:8

God Loves Me

Now our Lord Jesus Christ himself, and God, even our Father,
which hath loved us, and hath
given us everlasting consolation
and good hope through grace,
2 Thessalonians 2:16

Boldly Say: I am love by God, I
have nothing to worry about, God is
for me, I am never alone. The God
of consolation, is my God, God has
given me an everlasting consolation
in every situation, circumstances
and condition. I do have hope in
God in this present world, and I also

have eternal hope in God. My eternity is very secure in God, because I have accepted the full offering Jesus Christ made for me. Therefore, my eternity is secure, I do not and I must not, and I will not pay again what Jesus Christ my Saviour and Lord has paid.

Jeremiah 29:11
Romans 8:35-39

NOTE:

WEEK THIRTY-ONE

Love never fails:
1 Corinthians 13:8

God Loves Me

Nevertheless the LORD thy God would not hearken unto Balaam; but the LORD thy God turned the curse into a blessing unto thee, because the LORD thy God loved thee.

Deuteronomy 23:5

Boldly Say: **God will turn every negative word, every evil word and every negative emotion from anybody toward me into a blessing for me because God loves me. I am blessed of the Lord. The blessing of my Father God is in and on my life,**

the devil and his cohorts cannot curse who God has blessed. Curses are void and of non-effect upon me in any form, because I am redeemed from curses by the precious blood of Jesus Christ, who is my Saviour and Lord.

Jeremiah 29:11
Romans 8:35-39

NOTE:

WEEK THIRTY-TWO

Love never fails:
1 Corinthians 13:8

God Loves Me

Then Huram the king of Tyre answered in writing, which he sent to Solomon, Because the LORD hath loved his people, he hath made thee king over them.
2 Chronicles 2:11

Boldly Say: God loves me, God has given me excellent leadership because he loves me. I thank God for the leadership he has given me. I trust God that the leadership will do the will of God. Yes, they will governor in accordance to God's will. It is my responsibility to pray for them. I pray the blessing of my God will overtake them, and in his blessing they will acknowledge him.

Jeremiah 29:11
Romans 8:35-39

NOTE:

WEEK THIRTY-THREE

Love never fails:
1 Corinthians 13:8

God Loves Me

The LORD openeth the eyes of the blind: the LORD raiseth them that are bowed down: the LORD loveth the righteous:

Psalms 146:8

Boldly Say: God sent Jesus Christ to me because he loves me. The very moment I accepted Jesus Christ into my heart, God declared me righteous. God loves me, I am God's righteousness in Christ Jesus, my sins are forever forgiven by God Almighty, I do have peace with God, and I do have peace with myself. I do come to the throne of grace boldly at any time. My conscious is void of sin because Jesus Christ offered himself as the everlasting sacrifice to God for my sins. Jesus Christ was and is my Lamb. I love God, I love me, and I love people.

Jeremiah 29:11
Romans 8:35-39

NOTE:

WEEK THIRTY-FOUR

Love never fails:
1 Corinthians 13:8

God Loves Me

But after that the kindness and love of God our Saviour toward man appeared,
Titus 3:4

Boldly Say Father I thank you for your saving grace, for it is by your grace, I am saved, through faith. It was your love that brought your grace to me. Now that I am saved, your love is shed abroad in my heart by your Holy Spirit that dwells in me forever. God daily express his love through me to people. I do take the kindness and love of God to people. I communicate the love of God to people, telling people that because of the sacrifice Jesus Christ made to God for their sins, God is inviting each of them to come to him, God is not angry with anybody. Everyone can accept Jesus Christ as their sacrifice for their sins, everyone can be saved, Jesus Christ paid the price for everyone, Jesus Christ loves me, and he loves everybody.

Jeremiah 29:11
Romans 8:35-39

NOTE:

WEEK THIRTY-FIVE

Love never fails:
1 Corinthians 13:8

God Loves Me

But God commendeth his love toward us, in that, while we were yet sinners, Christ died for us.

Romans 5:8

Boldly Say: O the Love, the Love, the Love of God, beyond human comprehension. It is too great for any human intelligence. God loves me, this I know, and the death of Jesus Christ for sinners, forever settled any question about God's love. Who is he that condemn? Is Christ that died, ye, and yes, he arose from the grave, Amen Hallelujah forever.

I will never question the love of God for me and towards me, it is forever settled in my heart that I am love by God Almighty, whether the devil or anybody like it or not, love me or not, God loves me forever, I do love me. Amen.

Jeremiah 29:11
Romans 8:35-39

NOTE:

WEEK THIRTY-SIX

Love never fails:
1 Corinthians 13:8

God Loves Me

I will heal their backsliding, I will love them freely: for mine anger is turned away from him. Hosea 14:4

Boldly Say: Father I thank you that you never quit on me because you love me dearly. Whenever I miss the mark you always reach out to me in love, calling me to come back to you. I am forever grateful to you for your never quitting love for me and towards me all the time. When the evil one try to convince me that you are angry at me when I miss it, your Holy Spirit that dwells in me forever always assure me of the precious blood of Jesus Christ shed for me forever and also assure me of your great love for me. God loves me, I love God, I love me, and I love everyone.

Jeremiah 29:11
Romans 8:35-39

NOTE:

WEEK THIRTY-SEVEN

Love never fails:
1 Corinthians 13:8

God Loves Me

Nor height, nor depth, nor any other creature, shall be able to separate us from the love of God, which is in Christ Jesus our Lord.

Romans 8:39

Boldly Say: There is no success, there is no bad news, no denomination, no religious leader, no religious group or groups, no preacher, no board of any kind, and nobody, not even the devil or demons can separate me from the love of God Almighty, which is in Christ Jesus. No one or groups can vote me out of the love of God, because no one, no group or groups voted me into the love of God which is in Christ Jesus. God loves me and I love me, therefore, there is no debate about it. I am daily living in the love of God, and enjoying the love of God which is in Christ Jesus my Lord.

Jeremiah 29:11
Romans 8:35-39

NOTE:

WEEK THIRTY-EIGHT

Love never fails:
1 Corinthians 13:8

God Loves Me

For the love of Christ constrain-
eth us; because we thus judge,
that if one died for all, then were
all dead:

2 Corinthians 5:14

Boldly Say: Father I thank you
for your great love that has been
shed abroad in my heart, because of
your love in my heart, I am con-
strain from saying and doing anything that will not glorify you, build
me up, and build up people, whom
you made in your own image and
likeness, and whom Jesus Christ
died for to redeem with his precious

blood. The love of God shows me the way of grace. The love of God that constrained me makes me know that I am what I am because of the grace of God: that makes me to appreciate the love of God for me more every day.

Jeremiah 29:11
Romans 8:35-39

NOTE:

WEEK THIRTY-NINE

Love never fails:
1 Corinthians 13:8

God Loves Me

Husbands, love your wives, even as Christ also loved the church, and gave himself for it; **Ephesians 5:25**

Boldly Say: I am forever love by God. I thank you Father that divorce is never your will, therefore, I thank you that you will not let go of me, your love for me is an everlasting love, and our relationship is forever. God will never leave me nor forsake me; he said it and I do believe. Yes, God is always with me. Father, I thank you that you will not tell anyone to do what you have not destined them to do. Because you are love, I am love also, for I came from you.

Jeremiah 29:11
Romans 8:35-39

NOTE:

WEEK FORTY

Love never fails:
1 Corinthians 13:8

God Loves Me

Peace be to the brethren, and love with faith, from God the Father and the Lord Jesus Christ.

Ephesians 6:23

Boldly Say: Jesus I thank you for the peace that passes all understanding you have given to me. Yes, you are the Prince of peace, and you are my peace. Father I thank you that you do love me, and I thank you for your love for me. Yes, I am God's child and I am a child of faith. Therefore, God's love for me is not based on my feeling but on God's holy word, the Holy Bible. I boldly declare God loves me and I do love me regardless of how I feel, yes I love me unconditionally with the same love God have for me.

Jeremiah 29:11
Romans 8:35-39

NOTE:

WEEK FORTY-ONE

Love never fails:
1 Corinthians 13:8

God Loves Me

**And the Lord direct your hearts into the love of God, and into the patient waiting for Christ.
2 Thessalonians 3:5**

Boldly Say: **Father I thank you that Christ does dwell in my heart by faith, Lord Jesus I thank you that you are in my heart and you do direct my heart into the love of my Father. Therefore, I am consumed with the love of my Father, God Almighty. Yes, I do live, walk, breathe, and have my being in God's love. God's love is my current residence; anyone looking for me can find me**

in the love of God, while I am waiting on the return of my Lord and
Saviour Jesus Christ.

Jeremiah 29:11
Romans 8:35-39

NOTE:

WEEK FORTY-TWO

Love never fails:
1 Corinthians 13:8

God Loves Me

And the grace of our Lord was exceeding abundant with faith and love which is in Christ Jesus.

1 Timothy 1:14

Boldly Say: Father I thank you for your love in Christ for me, your grace that abound towards me. Father I thank you that your love brought your saving grace to me. Now that I am saved by grace through faith, and that it is not by my works, I boldly live in that grace by which I am saved, I will not go back to live in works. I will not live by religious do and do not, I will not live by denomination rules, I will not live by the traditions of men that make the word of God void of power. I will no longer live by my feelings, my strength or my power. Man shall not live by bread alone but by every word that proceed out of the mouth of the Living God. I do now live by the word of God Almighty.

Jeremiah 29:11
Romans 8:35-39

NOTE:

WEEK FORTY-THREE

Love never fails:
1 Corinthians 13:8

God Loves Me

Hold fast the form of sound words, which thou hast heard of me, in faith and love which is in Christ Jesus.
2 Timothy 1:13
Boldly Say: The word of God tells me who I am, what God has given to me, and what I can do through Christ Jesus. I do boldly live in the love of God for me, I do hold fast to his love for me. I do live in the love of God. Whenever I read the word of God, which I do read daily, I read it from the consciousness of the love of God for me, towards me and in

me. No, I do not read it from the consciousness of condemnation, because there is therefore, now no condemnation for me because I am in Christ Jesus. God loves me, I love me, and I love people.

Jeremiah 29:11
Romans 8:35-39

NOTE:

WEEK FORTY-FOUR

Love never fails:
1 Corinthians 13:8

God Loves Me

And we have known and be-
lieved the love that God hath to
us. God is love; and he that
dwelleth in love dwelleth in God,
and God in him.

1 John 4:16

Boldly Say: I do believe the love
God has for me, God declare his love
for me publicly, when he sent Jesus
Christ to die on the cross publicly
for me. Jesus Christ death on the
cross is the manifestation of God's
love for me and everyone. The love
of God for me was manifested in the

person of Jesus Christ. The love of God for me is real, yes it is tangible, and I know of a surety that God loves me. I do live in the love of God. God does live in me by his Holy Spirit that dwells in me forever.

Jeremiah 29:11
Romans 8:35-39

NOTE:

WEEK FORTY-FIVE

Love never fails:
1 Corinthians 13:8

God Loves Me

Hereby perceive we the love of God, because he laid down his life for us: and we ought to lay down our lives for the brethren. **1 John 3:16**

Boldly Say: God loves me greatly, and because he loves me, he came in the person of Jesus Christ and lay down his life for me. The fact that he laid down his life for me means I must be very valuable to him. He died that I might live, yes, and that I might have abundant life now, yes, to enjoy abundant life now, without any religion permission. Therefore, I go forth to live the life of Christ in the now. Yes, to walk as he walks. To live in the Christ lifestyle. He loves me, he died for me. I love him, I live for him.

Jeremiah 29:11
Romans 8:35-39

NOTE:

WEEK FORTY-SIX

Love never fails:
1 Corinthians 13:8

God Loves Me

Beloved, let us love one another: for love is of God; and every one that loveth is born of God, and knoweth God.

1 John 4:7

Boldly Say: God is Love. God is my Father and I am his child. Whatever is true of him is true of me. My Father loves me and I love my Father. As he is, so am I in this world. I came from love, I live in love, and my lifestyle is love. I am made from love, my substance is love, and therefore, I dare to think love thoughts. I dare to think God's thought about me.

I dare to see me as God sees me. I dare to think about people, as God thinks about people. I dare to see people as God sees people.
Love gives life, because life is in love.

Jeremiah 29:11
Romans 8:35-39

NOTE:

WEEK FORTY-SEVEN

Love never fails:
1 Corinthians 13:8

God Loves Me

He that loveth not knoweth not God; for God is love.
1 John 4:8

Boldly Say: I boldly acknowledge that God is my heavenly Father, just as Jesus Christ proceeded from the Father, so, have I proceeded from Jesus Christ. I am body of the body of Jesus Christ and bone of his bone. I am begotten by God through Jesus Christ, whatever is true of the Father, is true of the Son; whatever is true of the Son is true of me. The life which I do now live, I live by the faith of him, who loves me and gave his life for me.

I am called by God, I am anointed by God, I am sent by God, I am God's workmanship created in Christ Jesus, I am ambassador for Christ, I do go forth in Jesus name to share Jesus Christ with people and the Lord Jesus himself is always with me, confirming his word with signs following.

Jeremiah 29:11
Romans 8:35-39

NOTE:

WEEK FORTY-EIGHT

Love never fails:
1 Corinthians 13:8

God Loves Me

In this was manifested the love of God toward us, because that God sent his only begotten Son into the world, that we might live through him.

1 John 4:9

Boldly Say: The love of God for me has been shown publicly by Jesus Christ death on the cross publicly. Since, God has showed his love for me publicly, I go forth to show my love for God publicly and to live for him publicly. I am not ashamed of the gospel of Jesus Christ, for it is the power of God unto salvation to everyone that believes, for there is none other name under heaven given among men whereby we must be saved, in him I live, move and have my being.

Jeremiah 29:11
Romans 8:35-39

NOTE:

WEEK FORTY-NINE

Love never fails:
1 Corinthians 13:8

God Loves Me

Herein is love, not that we loved God, but that he loved us, and sent his Son to be the propitiation for our sins.

1 John 4:10

Boldly Say: While I was a sinner and rebelling against God's command without a cause, God still love me and demonstrate his love for me by sending Jesus Christ to die on the cross to pay the full price for my sins. God, I thank you for your great love for me. Since, God loves me dearly; I do love me, in spite of what religious folks may think of me. The

death of Jesus Christ for me, publicly announce his love for me to the
Heaven, to the Earth, and to the under the Earth. Yes, Jesus Christ also
announced his love for me and towards me to God, to the angels and
to all the devils which he defeated
forever for me.

Jeremiah 29:11
Romans 8:35-39

NOTE:

WEEK FIFTY

Love never fails:
1 Corinthians 13:8

God Loves Me

The grace of the Lord Jesus Christ, and the love of God, and the communion of the Holy Ghost, be with you all. Amen. **2 Corinthians 13:14**

Boldly Say: That God is always with me, is a fact that I cannot deny, regardless of my feelings, the devil cannot at any time persuade me to deny the ever presence of God with me. The devil and his cohorts know that I am born again and that Christ in me the hope of glory. In fact the devil does know that God loves me greatly and because the devil knows, the devil does hate me, but because I am in the love of God the wicked one cannot touch me.

Jeremiah 29:11
Romans 8:35-39

NOTE:

WEEK FIFTY-ONE

Love never fails:
1 Corinthians 13:8

God Loves Me

And from Jesus Christ, who is the faithful witness, and the first begotten of the dead, and the prince of the kings of the earth. Unto him that loved us, and washed us from our sins in his own blood,

Revelation 1:5

Boldly Say: Jesus Christ himself washed me from my sins with his own blood. Jesus Christ said "He that is washed needeth not save to wash his feet, but is clean every whit:", therefore, my sins are forever put away by the precious blood of Jesus Christ. I am forever forgiven; I do not have sin in me. Jesus Christ has washed me in his own precious blood because he loves me. Religious folks may want to argue and scream but I am who God says I am. I take God at his word. Let all men be liars, but God be Truth. If you denied him, He still abides faithful to the end. I boldly accept God and his word.

Jeremiah 29:11
Romans 8:35-39

NOTE:

WEEK FIFTY-TWO

Love never fails:
1 Corinthians 13:8

God Loves Me

Finally, brethren, farewell. Be perfect, be of good comfort, be of one mind, live in peace; and the God of love and peace shall be with you.

2 Corinthians 13:11

Boldly Say: God is Love, God through Jesus Christ gave me the assurance that he is with me always. Yes, the God of my Lord Jesus Christ will never leave me nor forsake me. His Holy Spirit is in me, does abide in me and with me forever, I cannot fail in life endeavor. He

always causes me to triumph. Yes,
greater is he that is in me, than he
that is in the world. No power or
force in the visible and invisible is
able to stop God and me, I am a
winner.
God loves me, I love me, and I love
people.

Jeremiah 29:11
Romans 8:35-39

NOTE:

SOIL Foundation, Inc.

All books can be purchase through amazon.com (search: OVBIJE BOOK)

Publication Books

All Day God

Praying the Word From the Book of Timothy

Praying the Word From the Book of Ephesians

Resurrection from the Flood

Coaching to Completion

Praying the Word From the Epistle of John

God Loves Me

Tracts:

5 Things God wants you to know

Love Yourself